SYMPHONIES
Nos. 4 and 7

ANTON BRUCKNER

SYMPHONIES
Nos. 4 and 7

in Full Score

Edited by Robert Haas
for the International Bruckner Society

DOVER PUBLICATIONS, INC., New York

This Dover edition, first published in 1990, is a republication
of portions of Volumes 4 and 7 from *Anton Bruckner: Sämtliche Werke. Kritische Gesamtausgabe*,
originally published by Bruckner-Verlag G.m.b.H., Leipzig, in 1936 and 1944;
Symphony no. 4 appears here in the form in which it was reprinted by
Vereinigung Volkseigener Verlage, Bruckner-Verlag, in 1952.
A table of contents, a glossary of German terms, and lists of instruments have been added,
and the introductory material by Robert Haas appears here in a new English translation.
The editorial notes (*Vorlagen-bericht*) have been omitted.

Manufactured in the United States of America
Dover Publications, Inc., 31 East 2nd Street, Mineola, N.Y. 11501

Library of Congress Cataloging-in-Publication Data

Bruckner, Anton, 1824–1896.
[Symphonies, no. 4, E♭ major]
Symphonies nos. 4 and 7.

In full score.
Reprint (1st work). Originally published: Leipzig :
Bruckner-Verlag, 1936. Originally published in series:
Sämtliche Werke / Anton Bruckner.
Reprint (2nd work). Originally published: Leipzig :
Bruckner-Verlag, 1944. Originally published in series:
Sämtliche Werke / Anton Bruckner.
Durations: ca. 1:00:00; ca. 1:08:00.
Includes English translations of the original German introductions.
1. Symphonies—Scores.   I. Haas, Robert, 1886–1960.
II. Bruckner, Anton, 1824–1896. Symphonies, no. 7, E major. 1990.
III. Internationale Bruckner-Gesellschaft.
M1001.B89   no. 4   1990   89-754722
ISBN 0-486-26262-6

CONTENTS

GLOSSARY OF GERMAN TERMS

anfangs, at the beginning
Anschwellung, crescendo

B, B-flat
bei, in
Besetzung, setting
bewegt, agitated, *bewegter,* more agitated
bis zum, until the
breit, broad, *breiter,* broader
Bruckners, Bruckner's (own)

das, the
der, the
deutlich, clearly
D. H., The Editor
die, the
doch, but

empfohlen, recommended
Es, E-flat
etwas, somewhat

feierlich, solemnly
fort u. fort, constantly

Gesangsperiode, songlike passage [mm. 93ff]
gesangvoll, songful, cantabile
gestrichen, bowed
geteilt, divisi
gezogen, drawn out, legato
gleicher, same

Hauptthema, main theme
hervortretend, prominent

im, in the
immer, always, becoming steadily
immer fort, immerfort, constantly
in, to, at

Jagdthema, hunting theme

keinesfalls, on no account
Klammern, parentheses

lang, long
länger, longer
langsam, slow, *langsamer,* slower

marcirt, markiert, emphatically, marcato
markig, emphatically, vigorously
mit, with

nach, (retunes) to
nicht, not
noch, still
Note, note

ohne, without

Partitur, score

recht, very
ruhig, peacefully, *ruhiger,* more peacefully

S., page
Saite, string
sanft, gently
schleppend, dragging

schnell, fast
schwer, heavily
sehr, very
selbst, himself
Spitze, tip of the bow
Spottvogel, mockingbird
Stärke, strength
steht, appears
Streicher, strings

Takt, measure
Teile, part
tief, low

u., und, and
über, over

vernehmbar, audibly
vgl., cf.
vier, four
Viertelnote, quarter-note

wie, as
wuchtig, vigorously, heavily

zu, too

1., 1tes, 1st
2te(s), 2nd
4tel, quarter

INTRODUCTION
(SYMPHONY NO. 4)

The present score corresponds with Anton Bruckner's autograph, which he bequeathed in his will *as the final version* to Vienna's imperial Hofbibliothek and today is preserved as manuscript 19476 in the music collection of the Nationalbibliothek in Vienna. In it the first three movements of the second version of this symphony (1878) are combined with the Finale in its third version (1880).

The same four movements were engraved and published as early as November 1889 by the publishing house of Albert J. Gutmann in Vienna. This first edition of the score, however, departs conspicuously from the text that is here made accessible for the first time. The changes include, along with confusing additions of tempo indications and questionable dynamic revisions, a thoroughgoing reorchestration of the entire symphony and serious meddling with the form of the Scherzo and Finale. The most important examples of the last type are the disturbing of the balance in the first Scherzo through premature interruption (at m. 250) and the addition of a diminuendo transition, and, further, the elimination of the beginning of the recapitulation in the Finale, where 48 measures (mm. 383–430) were omitted. In the first edition the recapitulation begins with the cantabile passage in D minor (12 measures), while in the autograph it appears transposed to F♯ minor.

Although it is certain that the first edition appeared in the master's lifetime, the circumstances that accompanied its publication can today no longer be verified. The draft mentioned above, in any case, takes absolutely no notice of the text of the first edition, which under closer investigation turns out to be a murky source for the specialist—that is, the result of the conception of practitioners about Bruckner. This represented a point of view whose justification appears to have been grounded in the special, unfavorable circumstances of the time of the publication, when inadequately developed orchestral technique, possibilities of performances only with orchestras of the second rank, and in general the limited power of comprehension of the listener had to be taken into consideration, but which today has been superseded, since it gave a different meaning to the well-considered and significant intent of its creator and must have been accepted by Bruckner as, at best, an unavoidable expedient. (The more detailed discussions of the difficult question of the sources are found in the source commentary. [The latter has been omitted from the Dover volume.])

This volume of the complete-works edition, which had to be divided into two half-volumes, thus does not contain the text of the first edition in its entirety; on the contrary, it provides the beautiful, unknown Finale of the second version of 1878 and the entire first version of the score of 1874. [*Note:* The Dover volume reproduces only the score as described in the first paragraph and published as an individual volume by the Bruckner-Verlag, that is, without the 1874 version of the symphony or the Finale of 1878.]

Vienna, February 1936   Professor Robert Haas

In addition to the editor, Siegmund von Hausegger and Elsa Krüger participated in the redaction of the score.
Duration: approx. 1 hour.

SYMPHONY NO. 4
INSTRUMENTATION

2 Flutes [Flöten, Fl.]
2 Oboes [Oboen, Ob.]
2 Clarinets (B♭) [Klarinetten in B, Klar.]
2 Bassoons [Fagotte, Fag.]
4 Horns (F) [Hörner in F, Hrn.]
3 Trumpets (F) [Trompeten in F, Tromp.]
3 Trombones (Alto, Tenor, Bass) [Posaunen (A. T. B.), Pos.]
Tuba [Bass-Tuba, B.-Tuba]
Timpani [Pauken, Pk.]
Violins I, II [Violine, Viol.]
Violas [Vla.]
Cellos [Violoncell, Vc.]
Basses [Kontrabass, Kb.]

SYMPHONY NO. 4 IN E-FLAT MAJOR ("ROMANTIC")

I

* (Klammern Bruckners)

44

II: ANDANTE

* (Klammern Bruckners)

III: SCHERZO

TRIO

IV: FINALE

*) (Klammern Bruckners)

*) (Klammern Bruckners)

INTRODUCTION
(SYMPHONY NO. 7)

The editing of the Seventh in the complete-works edition promised few surprises, since the first edition, published by Albert Gutmann, was engraved in 1885 following the master's autograph score, thus following the same source that was employed here, and it was said of the proofreading that it was very carefully supervised.

However, after close examination of the source, manuscript 19479 in the music division of the Nationalbibliothek in Vienna, it turned out that this generally accepted opinion was incorrect and was instead an unsupported prejudice. It rather allowed basic conceptions about Bruckner's character and works to be once more confirmed and verified. For that reason it soon became not simply a matter of correcting the numerous errors and inaccuracies that crept in in 1885 and had since attained the status of custom—firmly established wrong notes were clearly audible—but rather of also restoring the work's overall spirit, which had been harmed. Because, even in the Seventh, outside influence made itself felt appreciably in a work that had been composed in private, not only at the often-cited but heretofore never truly understood passage with the cymbal clash in the Adagio, but also in the instrumentation and indications, and in many large and small features.

In short, the autograph score is, in both its musical and its verbal text, full of additions in other hands; this outside participation could be ascertained in its details and determined in its larger significance, just as the deletions were able to be analyzed and deciphered, and only in that way could the original text be restored. The origin of and reason for the uncovered facts were easily revealed by reference to the circumstances surrounding the first performances; the evidence of the correspondence speaks plainly enough; the mystery of the cymbal clash was solved by Bruckner's own hand (see the illustration). On the burning question of contemporary performance practice and its relation to the Bruckner tradition, the notes written on the first-edition score by Dr. Carl Muck for himself were extremely rich and instructive. This working score of Muck's became, with his effects, the property of the music division of the Preussische Staatsbibliothek in Berlin; it was most courteously made available.

The large purpose here has been to pursue and complete the urgently needed demonstration of a more accurate assessment of Bruckner's spiritual evolution than has hitherto been known: the recognition of a fundamental truth that could only be openly represented, advocated, and certified in the complete-works edition, whereas it was previously not simply unnoticed but even completely twisted around. In brief, it is apparent that all the large works that Anton Bruckner created after finishing the Fifth Symphony came into being in completely integral form, with no self-doubt and without any changes after they were finished. The only exception, the first movement of the

Eighth, has a—today famous—tragic history. What is meant by the Fifth Symphony, however, is its true, unique form, which by now we are thoroughly familiar with, though it was entirely unknown—really buried—before its publication in the complete-works edition.

On this basis, it is now possible for experienced source criticism to recognize and eliminate outside additions; indeed, it is its duty to do so. Like the other symphonies, the Seventh was conceived and developed in superior, solitary effort; in this form it is here presented.

Vienna, August 1944   Professor Robert Haas

In addition to the editor, Elsa Krüger participated in the redaction of the score. Duration: approx. 68 minutes.

THE CYMBAL CLASH IN THE ADAGIO
Reproduction from the Autograph Score 19479

This strip (actual width: 30.4 cm.) is glued onto the right edge of the page with the letter W [page 220 in this volume] in such a way that it can be laid over the score and supplements it. In the score itself, staves for the triangle and cymbals are lacking not only on this page but throughout; moreover, in the whole Adagio, staves are lacking for the timpani. Only after the Leipzig or Munich performance, and before publication by Gutmann, was this strip inserted, with its addenda for timpani, triangle, and cymbals. It is an amazing calligraphic artwork, which Bruckner managed superbly; it combines the missing voices for the whole movement and at the same time forms the complete supplement of the score at the letter W.

But there are also private markings, which are easy to interpret—to the extent that one notices them. At the end of both the second and the third stave, hence at the end of the whole shortened score, Bruckner drew three question marks in ink, signifying that the entire addendum from the outset was doubtful sixfold. When the score was used as the engraving copy for the first edition, the question marks were crossed out in ink. But in contradiction to this, at the upper right of the strip, precisely above the spot that contains the shortened score for timpani, triangle, and cymbals, is a notation in pencil in the writing of Bruckner's old age; it limits itself to two words whose meaning is unmistakable, namely, "gilt nicht" [not valid].

Bruckner himself thus at the outset strongly threw in doubt (six question marks) the instrumental addendum represented by this strip, then finally completely withdrew it. The strip again attests that these instruments were originally completely absent from the score.

Symphony No. 7
Instrumentation

2 Flutes [Flöten, Fl.]

2 Oboes [Oboen, Ob.]

2 Clarinets (A) [Klarinetten in A, Klar.]

2 Bassoons [Fagotte, Fag.]

4 Horns (F) [Hörner in F, Hrn.]

3 Trumpets (F) [Trompeten in F, Tromp.]

3 Trombones (Alto, Tenor, Bass) [Posaunen (A. T. B.), Pos.]

2 Tenor (Wagner) Tubas (B♭) [Tenor-Tuben in B, Ten.-Tb.]

2 Bass (Wagner) Tubas (F) [Bass-Tuben in F, B.-Tb.]

Contrabass Tuba [Kontra-Basstuba, K.-Btb.]

Timpani [Pauken, Pk.]

Violins I, II [Violine, Viol.]

Violas [Vla.]

Cellos [Violoncell, Vc.]

Basses [Kontrabass, Kb.]

SYMPHONY NO. 7 IN E MAJOR

I

II: ANDANTE

sehr langsam *)

G Tempo I. Sehr langsam

(sehr langsam)

G (Tempo I. Sehr langsam)

sehr langsam

G (Tempo I. Sehr langsam)

(*) vgl. ritardando S.62, Takt 153.   D.H.)

204

NB. 2te Trompete und 1tes u. 2tes Horn immer marcirt bis zum Legato

*)(Bruckner hat selbst die Besetzung mit vier Hörnern empfohlen. D.H.)

Symphony No. 7 (II)   223

III: SCHERZO

NB. Spottvogel (steht über der Partitur. D.H.)

Symphony No. 7 (III)   235

TRIO

Scherzo Da Capo

IV: FINALE

Symphony No. 7 (IV)   253

Dover Orchestral Scores

THE SIX BRANDENBURG CONCERTOS AND THE FOUR ORCHESTRAL SUITES IN FULL SCORE, Johann Sebastian Bach. Complete standard Bach-Gesellschaft editions in large, clear format. Study score. 273pp. 9 × 12. 23376-6 Pa. **$10.95**

COMPLETE CONCERTI FOR SOLO KEYBOARD AND ORCHESTRA IN FULL SCORE, Johann Sebastian Bach. Bach's seven complete concerti for solo keyboard and orchestra in full score from the authoritative Bach-Gesellschaft edition. 206pp. 9 × 12. 24929-8 Pa. **$9.95**

THE THREE VIOLIN CONCERTI IN FULL SCORE, Johann Sebastian Bach. Concerto in A Minor, BWV 1041; Concerto in E Major, BWV 1042; and Concerto for Two Violins in D Minor, BWV 1043. Bach-Gesellschaft edition. 64pp. 9⅜ × 12¼. 25124-1 Pa. **$5.95**

GREAT ORGAN CONCERTI, OPP. 4 & 7, IN FULL SCORE, George Frideric Handel. 12 organ concerti composed by great Baroque master are reproduced in full score from the *Deutsche Handelgesellschaft* edition. 138pp. 9⅜ × 12¼. 24462-8 Pa. **$7.95**

COMPLETE CONCERTI GROSSI IN FULL SCORE, George Frideric Handel. Monumental Opus 6 Concerti Grossi, Opus 3 and "Alexander's Feast" Concerti Grossi—19 in all—reproduced from most authoritative edition. 258pp. 9⅜ × 12¼. 24187-4 Pa. **$11.95**

COMPLETE CONCERTI GROSSI IN FULL SCORE, Arcangelo Corelli. All 12 concerti in the famous late nineteenth-century edition prepared by violinist Joseph Joachim and musicologist Friedrich Chrysander. 240pp. 8⅜ × 11¼. 25606-5 Pa. **$11.95**

WATER MUSIC AND MUSIC FOR THE ROYAL FIREWORKS IN FULL SCORE, George Frideric Handel. Full scores of two of the most popular Baroque orchestral works performed today—reprinted from definitive Deutsche Handelgesellschaft edition. Total of 96pp. 8⅜ × 11. 25070-9 Pa. **$5.95**

LATER SYMPHONIES, Wolfgang A. Mozart. Full orchestral scores to last symphonies (Nos. 35-41) reproduced from definitive Breitkopf & Härtel Complete Works edition. Study score. 285pp. 9 × 12. 23052-X Pa. **$11.95**

17 DIVERTIMENTI FOR VARIOUS INSTRUMENTS, Wolfgang A. Mozart. Sparkling pieces of great vitality and brilliance from 1771-1779; consecutively numbered from 1 to 17. Reproduced from definitive Breitkopf & Härtel Complete Works edition. Study score. 241pp. 9⅜ × 12¼. 23862-8 Pa. **$11.95**

PIANO CONCERTOS NOS. 11-16 IN FULL SCORE, Wolfgang Amadeus Mozart. Authoritative Breitkopf & Härtel edition of six staples of the concerto repertoire, including Mozart's cadenzas for Nos. 12-16. 256pp. 9⅜ × 12¼. 25468-2 Pa. **$11.95**

PIANO CONCERTOS NOS. 17-22, Wolfgang Amadeus Mozart. Six complete piano concertos in full score, with Mozart's own cadenzas for Nos. 17-19. Breitkopf & Härtel edition. Study score. 370pp. 9⅜ × 12¼. 23599-8 Pa. **$14.95**

PIANO CONCERTOS NOS. 23-27, Wolfgang Amadeus Mozart. Mozart's last five piano concertos in full score, plus cadenzas for Nos. 23 and 27, and the Concert Rondo in D Major, K.382. Breitkopf & Härtel edition. Study score. 310pp. 9⅜ × 12¼. 23600-5 Pa. **$11.95**

CONCERTI FOR WIND INSTRUMENTS IN FULL SCORE, Wolfgang Amadeus Mozart. Exceptional volume contains ten pieces for orchestra and wind instruments and includes some of Mozart's finest, most popular music. 272pp. 9⅜ × 12¼. 25228-0 Pa. **$12.95**

THE VIOLIN CONCERTI AND THE SINFONIA CONCERTANTE, K.364, IN FULL SCORE, Wolfgang Amadeus Mozart. All five violin concerti and famed double concerto reproduced from authoritative Breitkopf & Härtel Complete Works Edition. 208pp. 9⅜ × 12½. 25169-1 Pa. **$10.95**

SYMPHONIES 88-92 IN FULL SCORE: The Haydn Society Edition, Joseph Haydn. Full score of symphonies Nos. 88 through 92. Large, readable noteheads, ample margins for fingerings, etc., and extensive Editor's Commentary. 304pp. 9 × 12. (Available in U.S. only) 24445-8 Pa. **$13.95**

COMPLETE LONDON SYMPHONIES IN FULL SCORE, Series I and Series II, Joseph Haydn. Reproduced from the Eulenburg editions are Symphonies Nos. 93-98 (Series I) and Nos. 99-104 (Series II). 800pp. 8⅜ × 11¼. (Available in U.S. only)
Series I 24982-4 Pa. **$14.95**
Series II 24983-2 Pa. **$15.95**

FOUR SYMPHONIES IN FULL SCORE, Franz Schubert. Schubert's four most popular symphonies: No. 4 in C Minor ("Tragic"); No. 5 in B-flat Major; No. 8 in B Minor ("Unfinished"); and No. 9 in C Major ("Great"). Breitkopf & Härtel edition. Study score. 261pp. 9⅜ × 12¼. 23681-1 Pa. **$11.95**

GREAT OVERTURES IN FULL SCORE, Carl Maria von Weber. Overtures to *Oberon, Der Freischutz, Euryanthe* and *Preciosa* reprinted from authoritative Breitkopf & Härtel editions. 112pp. 9 × 12. 25225-6 Pa. **$6.95**

SYMPHONIES NOS. 1, 2, 3, AND 4 IN FULL SCORE, Ludwig van Beethoven. Republication of H. Litolff edition. 272pp. 9 × 12. 26033-X Pa. **$10.95**

SYMPHONIES NOS. 5, 6 AND 7 IN FULL SCORE, Ludwig van Beethoven. Republication of the H. Litolff edition. 272pp. 9 × 12. 26034-8 Pa. **$10.95**

SYMPHONIES NOS. 8 AND 9 IN FULL SCORE, Ludwig van Beethoven. Republication of the H. Litolff edition. 256pp. 9 × 12. 26035-6 Pa. **$10.95**

SIX GREAT OVERTURES IN FULL SCORE, Ludwig van Beethoven. Six staples of the orchestral repertoire from authoritative Breitkopf & Härtel edition. *Leonore Overtures*, Nos. 1-3; Overtures to *Coriolanus, Egmont, Fidelio.* 288pp. 9 × 12. 24789-9 Pa. **$12.95**

COMPLETE PIANO CONCERTOS IN FULL SCORE, Ludwig van Beethoven. Complete scores of five great Beethoven piano concertos, with all cadenzas as he wrote them, reproduced from authoritative Breitkopf & Härtel edition. New table of contents. 384pp. 9⅜ × 12¼. 24563-2 Pa. **$14.95**

GREAT ROMANTIC VIOLIN CONCERTI IN FULL SCORE, Ludwig van Beethoven, Felix Mendelssohn and Peter Ilyitch Tchaikovsky. The Beethoven Op. 61, Mendelssohn, Op. 64 and Tchaikovsky, Op. 35 concertos reprinted from the Breitkopf & Härtel editions. 224pp. 9 × 12. 24989-1 Pa. **$10.95**

MAJOR ORCHESTRAL WORKS IN FULL SCORE, Felix Mendelssohn. Generally considered to be Mendelssohn's finest orchestral works, here in one volume are: the complete *Midsummer Night's Dream; Hebrides Overture; Calm Sea and Prosperous Voyage Overture;* Symphony No. 3 in A ("Scottish"); and Symphony No. 4 in A ("Italian"). Breitkopf & Härtel edition. Study score. 406pp. 9 × 12. 23184-4 Pa. **$15.95**

COMPLETE SYMPHONIES, Johannes Brahms. Full orchestral scores. No. 1 in C Minor, Op. 68; No. 2 in D Major, Op. 73; No. 3 in F Major, Op. 90; and No. 4 in E Minor, Op. 98. Reproduced from definitive Vienna Gesellschaft der Musikfreunde edition. Study score. 344pp. 9 × 12. 23053-8 Pa. **$13.95**

Dover Orchestral Scores

THREE ORCHESTRAL WORKS IN FULL SCORE: Academic Festival Overture, Tragic Overture and Variations on a Theme by Joseph Haydn, Johannes Brahms. Reproduced from the authoritative Breitkopf & Härtel edition three of Brahms's great orchestral favorites. Editor's commentary in German and English. 112pp. 9⅜ × 12¼. 24637-X Pa. **$8.95**

COMPLETE CONCERTI IN FULL SCORE, Johannes Brahms. Piano Concertos Nos. 1 and 2; Violin Concerto, Op. 77; Concerto for Violin and Cello, Op. 102. Definitive Breitkopf & Härtel edition. 352pp. 9⅜ × 12¼. 24170-X Pa. **$14.95**

COMPLETE SYMPHONIES IN FULL SCORE, Robert Schumann. No. 1 in B-flat Major, Op. 38 ("Spring"); No. 2 in C Major, Op. 61; No. 3 in E Flat Major, Op. 97 ("Rhenish"); and No. 4 in D Minor, Op. 120. Breitkopf & Härtel editions. Study score. 416pp. 9⅜ × 12¼. 24013-4 Pa. **$16.95**

GREAT WORKS FOR PIANO AND ORCHESTRA IN FULL SCORE, Robert Schumann. Collection of three superb pieces for piano and orchestra, including the popular Piano Concerto in A Minor. Breitkopf & Härtel edition. 183pp. 9⅜ × 12¼. 24340-0 Pa. **$9.95**

THE PIANO CONCERTOS IN FULL SCORE, Frédéric Chopin. The authoritative Breitkopf & Härtel full-score edition in one volume of Piano Concertos No. 1 in E Minor and No. 2 in F Minor. 176pp. 9 × 12. 25835-1 Pa. **$8.95**

THE PIANO CONCERTI IN FULL SCORE, Franz Liszt. Available in one volume the Piano Concerto No. 1 in E-flat Major and the Piano Concerto No. 2 in A Major—are among the most studied, recorded and performed of all works for piano and orchestra. 144pp. 9 × 12. 25221-3 Pa. **$7.95**

SYMPHONY NO. 8 IN G MAJOR, OP. 88, SYMPHONY NO. 9 IN E MINOR, OP. 95 ("NEW WORLD") IN FULL SCORE, Antonín Dvořák. Two celebrated symphonies by the great Czech composer, the Eighth and the immensely popular Ninth, "From the New World" in one volume. 272pp. 9 × 12. 24749-X Pa. **$11.95**

FOUR ORCHESTRAL WORKS IN FULL SCORE: Rapsodie Espagnole, Mother Goose Suite, Valses Nobles et Sentimentales, and Pavane for a Dead Princess, Maurice Ravel. Four of Ravel's most popular orchestral works, reprinted from original full-score French editions. 240pp. 9⅜ × 12¼. (Not available in France or Germany) 25962-5 Pa. **$10.95**

DAPHNIS AND CHLOE IN FULL SCORE, Maurice Ravel. Definitive full-score edition of Ravel's rich musical setting of a Greek fable by Longus is reprinted here from the original French edition. 320pp. 9⅜ × 12¼. (Not available in France or Germany) 25826-2 Pa. **$14.95**

THREE GREAT ORCHESTRAL WORKS IN FULL SCORE, Claude Debussy. Three favorites by influential modernist: *Prélude à l'Après-midi d'un Faune, Nocturnes,* and *La Mer.* Reprinted from early French editions. 279pp. 9 × 12. 24441-5 Pa. **$11.95**

SYMPHONY IN D MINOR IN FULL SCORE, César Franck. Superb, authoritative edition of Franck's only symphony, an often-performed and recorded masterwork of late French romantic style. 160pp. 9 × 12. 25373-2 Pa. **$8.95**

THE GREAT WALTZES IN FULL SCORE, Johann Strauss, Jr. Complete scores of eight melodic masterpieces: The Beautiful Blue Danube, Emperor Waltz, Tales of the Vienna Woods, Wiener Blut, four more. Authoritative editions. 336pp. 8⅜ × 11¼. 26009-7 Pa. **$12.95**

FOURTH, FIFTH AND SIXTH SYMPHONIES IN FULL SCORE, Peter Ilyitch Tchaikovsky. Complete orchestral scores of Symphony No. 4 in F minor, Op. 36; Symphony No. 5 in E minor, Op. 64; Symphony No. 6 in B minor, "Pathetique," Op. 74. Study score. Breitkopf & Härtel editions. 480pp. 9⅜ × 12¼. 23861-X Pa. **$18.95**

ROMEO AND JULIET OVERTURE AND CAPRICCIO ITALIEN IN FULL SCORE, Peter Ilyitch Tchaikovsky. Two of Russian master's most popular compositions in high quality, inexpensive reproduction. From authoritative Russian edition. 208pp. 8⅝ × 11½. 25217-5 Pa. **$8.95**

NUTCRACKER SUITE IN FULL SCORE, Peter Ilyitch Tchaikovsky. Among the most popular ballet pieces ever created—a complete, inexpensive, high-quality score to study and enjoy. 128pp. 9 × 12. 25379-1 Pa. **$6.95**

TONE POEMS, SERIES I: DON JUAN, TOD UND VERKLARUNG, and DON QUIXOTE, Richard Strauss. Three of the most often performed and recorded works in entire orchestral repertoire, reproduced in full score from original editions. Study score. 286pp. 9⅜ × 12¼. (Available in U.S. only) 23754-0 Pa. **$13.95**

TONE POEMS, SERIES II: TILL EULENSPIEGELS LUSTIGE STREICHE, ALSO SPRACH ZARATHUSTRA, and EIN HELDENLEBEN, Richard Strauss. Three important orchestral works, including very popular *Till Eulenspiegel's Merry Pranks,* reproduced in full score from original editions. Study score. 315pp. 9⅜ × 12¼. (Available in U.S. only) 23755-9 Pa. **$13.95**

DAS LIED VON DER ERDE IN FULL SCORE, Gustav Mahler. Mahler's masterpiece, a fusion of song and symphony, reprinted from the original 1912 Universal Edition. English translations of song texts. 160pp. 9 × 12. 25657-X Pa. **$8.95**

SYMPHONIES NOS. 1 AND 2 IN FULL SCORE, Gustav Mahler. Unabridged, authoritative Austrian editions of Symphony No. 1 in D Major ("Titan") and Symphony No. 2 in C Minor ("Resurrection"). 384pp. 8¼ × 11. 25473-9 Pa. **$14.95**

SYMPHONIES NOS. 3 AND 4 IN FULL SCORE, Gustav Mahler. Two brilliantly contrasting masterworks—one scored for a massive ensemble, the other for small orchestra and soloist—reprinted from authoritative Viennese editions. 368pp. 9⅜ × 12¼. 26166-2 Pa. **$14.95**

SYMPHONY NO. 8 IN FULL SCORE, Gustav Mahler. Superb authoritative edition of massive, complex "Symphony of a Thousand." Scored for orchestra, eight solo voices, double chorus, boys' choir and organ. Reprint of Izdatel'stvo "Muzyka," Moscow, edition. Translation of texts. 272pp. 9⅜ × 12¼. 26022-4 Pa. **$11.95**

THE FIREBIRD IN FULL SCORE (Original 1910 Version), Igor Stravinsky. Handsome, inexpensive edition of modern masterpiece, renowned for brilliant orchestration, glowing color. Authoritative Russian edition. 176pp. 9⅜ × 12¼. (Available in U.S. only) 25535-2 Pa. **$9.95**

PETRUSHKA IN FULL SCORE: Original Version, Igor Stravinsky. The definitive full-score edition of Stravinsky's masterful score for the great Ballets Russes 1911 production of *Petrushka.* 160pp. 9⅜ × 12¼. (Available in U.S. only) 25680-4 Pa. **$9.95**

THE RITE OF SPRING IN FULL SCORE, Igor Stravinsky. A reprint of the original full-score edition of the most famous musical work of the 20th century, created as a ballet score for Diaghilev's Ballets Russes. 176pp. 9⅜ × 12¼. (Available in U.S. only) 25857-2 Pa. **$9.95**

*Available from your music dealer or write for **free** Music Catalog to Dover Publications, Inc., Dept. MUBI, 31 East 2nd Street, Mineola, N.Y. 11501.*